CITY WORKERS

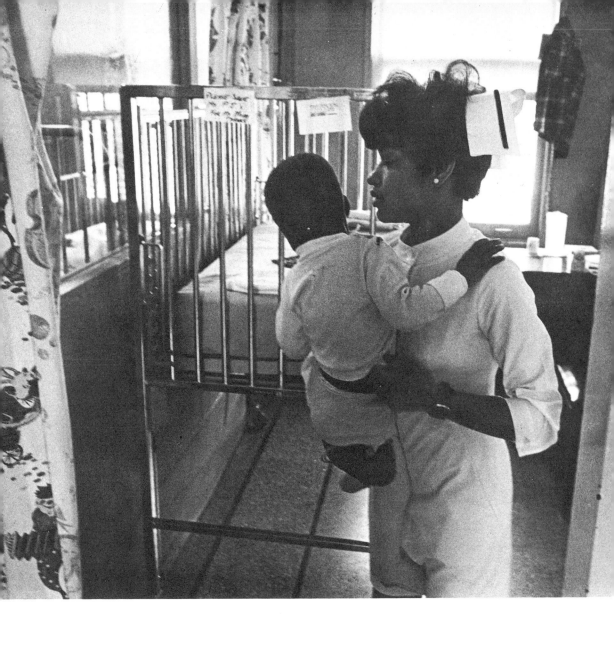

City Visits

CITY
WORKERS

Jeanne A. Rowe

LIBRARY EDITION 1970
RESPONSIVE ENVIRONMENTS CORP.
Englewood Cliffs, N.J. 07632

Franklin Watts, Inc.

575 Lexington Avenue   New York, N.Y. 10022

photo credits

Hermann Bachmann: pages 2, 6, 15, 17, 19, 29, 35, 43, 45 and 46.
Bob Clark: pages 10, 21, 22, 24, 27, 30, 32, 37 and 40.
New York Fire Department: page 9.
AT & T Photo Service: page 38.

CITY WORKERS

THE POLICEMAN

Work is an important part of living. We work to make money for a home, food, and clothing for our families. Some workers produce goods. Some workers provide services. Many of the services performed are for all the people of the city. We pay for them by taxes.

Taxes pay for the services of the policeman. Policemen often go around the neighborhood in a patrol car. A two-way radio in the car tells them where help is needed. When they are in a hurry, a red flashing light and a screeching siren on the top of the car tell people and other cars to get out of the way.

THE FIREMAN

All day and all night firemen are on
duty to help put out fires. They
wear rubber boots and coats to
protect them from cold, heat, and
water. Heavy canvas gloves protect
them from splinters and nails. A
leather helmet keeps water away
from their eyes and necks, and
breaks the shock of falling objects.
Fire hydrants connected to the city
water supply are placed a few
hundred feet apart on each street.
The pressure of the rushing water
from these hydrants is strong, and
at least three men must hold the
hose when water is coming through.

New York Fire Department

THE SANITATION WORKER

Sanitation workers have a big job to do. Garbage has to be picked up often. Most garbage is left in metal cans that do not leak. The loaders take the covers off and empty the cans into the hopper at the back of the truck. They wear heavy gloves so their hands will not be cut by any jagged edges on the cans or by broken glass. A machine in the back of the truck pushes the garbage forward and packs it. Then the truck is driven first to a furnace where the garbage is burned, and then to a landfill site where the ashes are buried. This land may someday become an airport or a park.

THE POSTMAN

One of the best-liked public workers
is the postman. The postman does
many different types of jobs. Most
postmen go around the same
neighborhood every day. The
postman may pick up the mail
that we have put in the mailbox
on the corner, or he may deliver
mail to homes and offices. At the
post office, mail is sorted by zip
codes. The zip code has five
numbers. People write the zip code
on letters and packages to help
show the post-office worker exactly
where the mail is going.

THE DOCTOR

When we are sick we go to the doctor to find out what is wrong. To begin with, the doctor checks the patient's heartbeat with his stethoscope. The stethoscope is an instrument used for listening to the sounds produced in the body, especially in the chest. In hospitals doctors wear white jackets with little name-tags on them. If someone telephones the doctor or if he is needed for an emergency, his name is called out on a loudspeaker.

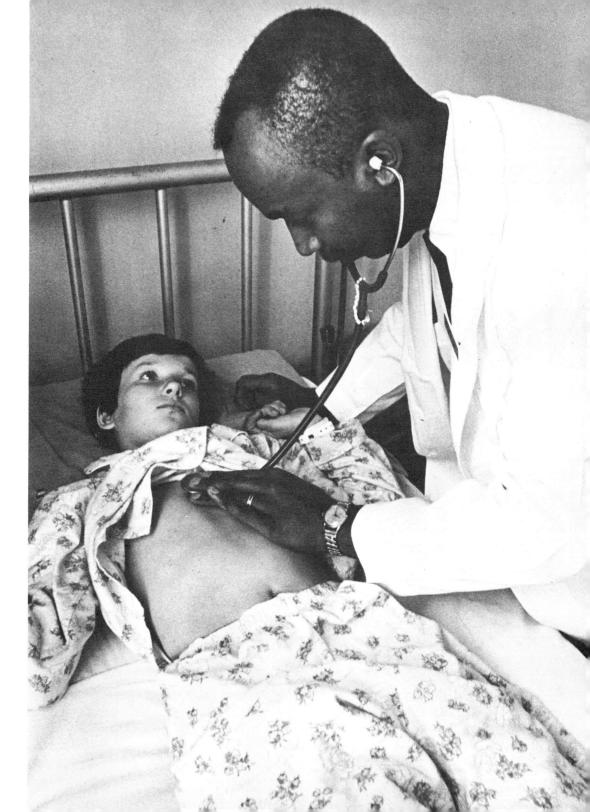

THE NURSE

Since the doctor cannot always stay with patients, workers called nurses are there to see that everything is all right. They keep records on the patients' care and bring them things which they cannot get for themselves. Nurses sometimes bring juice to a patient who is too young to get down from his high chair. The hospital room may have a television set and toys in it. You can tell who the nurse is because she is always dressed all in white — a white cap, a white dress, white stockings, and white shoes.

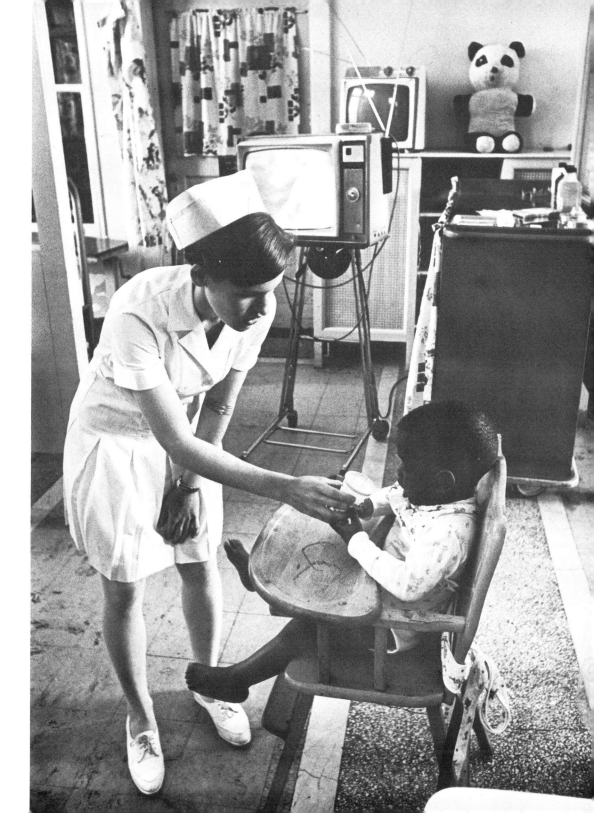

THE DENTIST and
THE DENTAL NURSE

Everyone should take good care of
his teeth and should visit the
dentist. The dentist is an important
worker and so is the dental nurse
who stands by to help him. By
putting a small mirror in the
patient's mouth, the dentist can see
all sides of the teeth. A bright light
from above shines on the patient,
and this also helps the dentist to
see if there are any cavities.

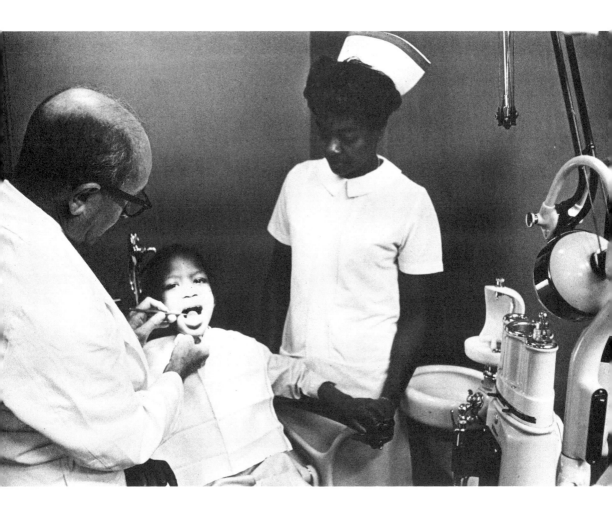

THE SCHOOLTEACHER

In some classes the schoolteacher might teach everything, in others he might teach only reading or arithmetic. One way to learn how to read well is to say the words along with the teacher. Another way is to study the letters and words on the bulletin board. Besides teaching reading, a teacher might take the class to the cafeteria for lunch or to the playground for games.

THE LIBRARIAN

Almost everybody likes to go to the public library. At the library there is a librarian who helps people find the kind of books they like. She will show them how to borrow books and tell them when they must be brought back. And on many days, the librarian will have a special reading-hour for the children of the neighborhood. She tells an exciting tale and shows off the beautiful pictures in the book. Sometimes she will ask her listeners to tell her what they like best about the story.

THE CASHIER

Supermarkets service city people by buying food from factories and farms, so they can sell it to their customers. There are many kinds of workers at the supermarket, but the one you meet most often is the cashier. The cashier looks to see how much the food costs and rings up the price of each item on the cash register. The register adds up all the prices and shows how much the customer must pay. People shop at the supermarket because it has so many things they need — meat and fish, fruits and vegetables, bread and cookies, and many other things.

THE SHOE SALESMAN

People need clothes for work and
school. The department store carries
many types and sizes of clothing.
Before school starts we may need
a new pair of shoes. Perhaps we
have grown and our old pair no
longer fits. The shoe salesman
measures our feet to see what size
is the right size for us. He brings
out a box with new shoes that must
be tried on. If you like them and
they feel good, Mother will
probably buy them.

THE ARCHITECT and
CITY PLANNER

When we want to make our
neighborhoods better, we choose
someone to plan the way to do it.
Sometimes buildings are torn down
to make way for new ones.
Sometimes the old ones will be
repainted. An architect and city
planner makes drawings of how a
neighborhood should look. He
shows where we might put the
supermarket, the school, the church,
the synagogue, and the playground.
He tries to find out what the
people want and how much it will
cost. He might make a model of
what the apartment house would
look like if it were built.

THE GAS and
ELECTRICITY REPAIRMAN

In a city every house needs
electricity for light; some need gas
for cooking. Pipes and wires under
the ground bring gas and
electricity to each house. If a pipe
has broken, a repair crew must
go underground to fix it. The
repairman in the background is
breaking up the pavement with a
drill. He is wearing safety goggles
to protect his eyes. The two other
repair workers are shoveling out
the loosened pavement. They are
wearing heavy gloves and helmets.
The work area is surrounded by
white safety-tape and red warning-
flags.

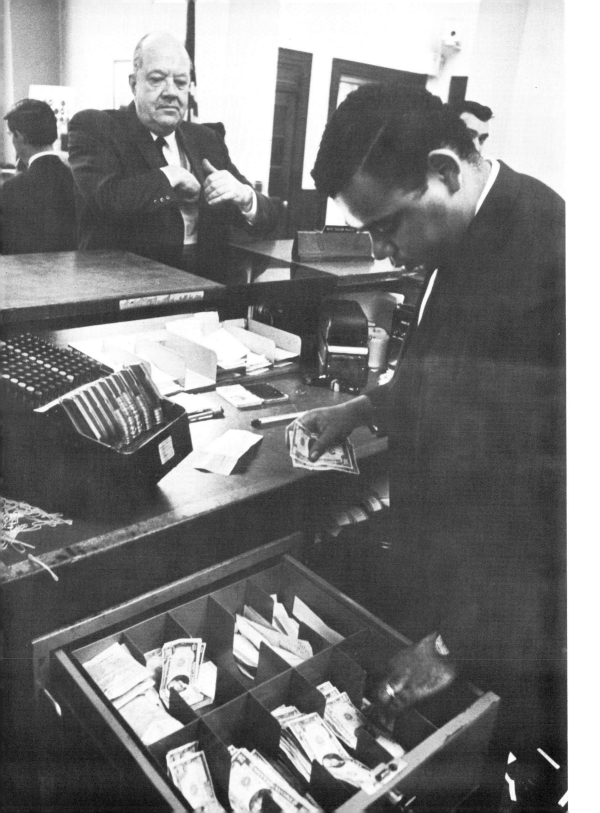

THE BANK TELLER

To buy things in stores you need money. Most people keep their money in a bank. A bank offers many services. It keeps people's money safe. It lends money for opening a business or buying a house. Behind the counter at the bank is a bank teller. He is cashing a customer's check. The check shows the teller how much the customer wants to take out from his savings.

THE PAINTER

The walls of a building
   often need a fresh coat of paint.
   The painter wears work clothes to
   protect his body from the paint,
   which sometimes drips. When he
   paints in your house he covers the
   furniture with a heavy cloth.
   Painters use a paintbrush, but
   sometimes for the large areas they
   use a roller. After the roller is
   dipped in a pan of paint, it is
   rolled up and down the wall.

STEP DOWN

THE FACTORY WORKER

Many jobs in big cities are service
jobs. But many are also at factories
or places where goods are made.
In factories each worker does a
special job. Here, in a pot-and-pan
factory, a worker stands in front
of the machine he runs. He wears
rubber gloves to protect his hands.
The machine stamps a flat piece of
metal into the shape of a pan.
Then each pan is put on a belt
that carries it to other workers, one
after the other. One worker will
put on the handle. Another will
polish the pan. When it is finished
it will be sent to a packer who
will put it in a box.

THE TELEPHONE OPERATOR

People like to call their friends and
family on the telephone when they
are not nearby. Stores need the
telephone to call customers. The
person who helps you place a call
is the telephone operator. You dial
"O" on the telephone when you
want to get the operator to make
an emergency call to the police,
the firemen, or a hospital. These
operators are using a new
pushbutton machine to help callers
get faster service.

New York Telephone Co.

THE FILE CLERK

Most stores and businesses have
offices that keep important papers.
Some are letters from customers.
Others are bills from the people
who send them food or materials.
Still others are order slips that give
the name and address of the
customer, the object purchased,
and the price. File clerks make
sure that the papers are put in the
right order so that when someone
wants them they can be found
quickly. Keeping these papers neat
and in a special order must be
done by any business that wants
to do well.

THE EMPLOYMENT COUNSELOR

How do workers find the right jobs?

An employment counselor helps people find the right jobs. The counselor writes on a form the number of years the person has gone to school, the extra training he has had, and the kind of job he would like best. We need employment counselors because the city is so large and there are so many different types of workers needed. Other ways to find jobs are to look at job advertisements in the newspaper or to go right to the company or store manager.

THE LAUNDRY ATTENDANT

Sometimes mothers cannot wait while
the wash is being done at the
automatic laundry. Sometimes they
might have to go to work or go
shopping. So they leave their wash
with the laundry attendant. The
laundry attendant will put the
laundry in the machine and then
fold it up when it is dry. She
returns the laundry to the customer
in a large white laundry-bag. She
calls on the telephone to order
more soap. Imagine how hard it
used to be before there were
machines and Mother had to do
all the wash by hand.

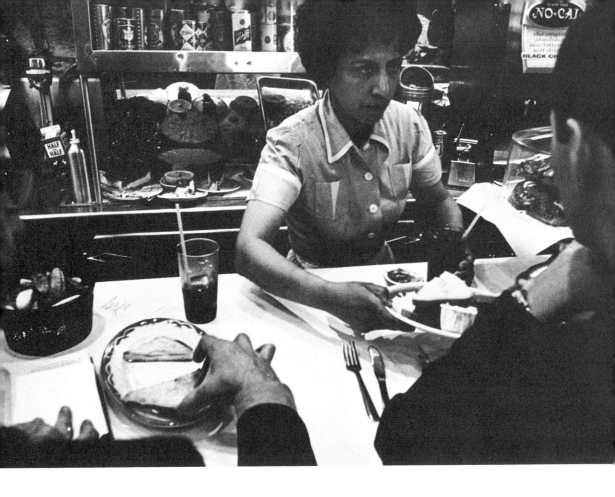

THE WAITRESS

When we are hungry and are not near home, we go to a diner or restaurant. At the counter a waitress serves us. The menu tells us what dishes the restaurant prepares and how much we will have to pay for each one. After you tell the waitress what you would like to order, she tells the cook. When the dish you have ordered is ready, the waitress brings it to your place at the counter or table.

These are just a few of the many, many different types of workers we find in the city. How many more can you think of?

DATE DUE

FORM 393 SCHOOL SPECIALTY SUPPLY, SALINA, KANSAS